Hecate

Safienaaz Chughtai

Presentation by *BookLeaf Publishing*

Web: www.bookleafpub.com

E-mail: info@bookleafpub.com

ISBN: 978-93-95784-86-3

First edition 2022

For my parents, Zuleika and Saashah who have guided and encouraged me every step of the way.

For my brother, Rayaan who is my inspiration and moral compass.

For my grandparents, especially my late grandfather, Arshad Sethi who taught me the art of story telling.

PREFACE

As a young child, I expressed my emotions via drawing. My mother recounts an incident where I, as a three year old, upset after being scolded for misbehaving, went into a corner and quietly drew a heart that was broken in two. I then scribbled what I thought was, "My heart is broken into pieces"

As I grew older, amongst a family of avid readers and heated colorful discussions about various books and plays, I began to appreciate the power of the written word and how it transported you from rapture to despair in a matter of seconds. I understood then that words could evoke powerful emotions and memories - and that all creativity came from the word itself.

When Covid hit the world, my life changed as well. Growing up as an expat in different countries, my sense of identity and grounding came from the long lazy summers spent in my grandparents' house in Pakistan.

The sights, tastes, smells and experiences of family gatherings and feasts of deeply fried spicy food and cool almond sherbet as we enjoyed the monsoon rains, became an integral part of my childhood and formative years. The most precious and valuable time however was the story telling sessions we had most evenings gathered together next to my grandmother, Ami, as she conjured up fascinating tales of the women of our family line.

These were stories of strong beautiful resilient women who had worked hard, travelled across continents in the wake of the bloody partition of India and Pakistan, while keeping their grace and dignity.

These stories often ended with my late grandfather making some funny remark about the main character and then he would recite a poetic verse, sometimes in English and sometimes in Urdu.
Wide eyed, I would listen trying to grasp every word, and thus began my love affair with writing.

With Covid lockdowns, I lost my summers in Pakistan and I lost my grandfather.

These poems are a tribute to my heritage, of strength, resilience, love, loss and of rising again amidst adversity.
Hecate is the beautiful goddess signifying love and innocence: the nourisher and home maker. Finally, the guide and the wisdom we accrue as we embark on the journey of life.

The Maiden

Loving you is like loving a book.
There will be ups, and there will be downs,
There will be peaks of motivation and times of distress,
But no matter how many times I read this book,
It will always come to an end.

Your smile seems to be the remedy to
all of my diseases.
No matter how bad it gets, you never
fail to cure me.
Except for one.
The fatal fear of losing you;
The fear that my smile may not be the
remedy to all of your diseases.

I stood, watching.
Watching a chrysanthemum.
The chrysanthemum's petals were
starting to crisp:
The pink to a brown.
I went over,
And tried taking it.
It stayed with the others.
I tried again, but a bit harder this
time.
Still nothing.
I then understood,
Then told it,
That my petals are starting to crisp as well,
But just because they're brown now,
Doesn't mean it won't be pink later.
And with this, I gently plucked it,
And began the journey up the steps.

I always loved lighting,
It never scared me.
In fact, it brought me comfort
Because whenever I saw it,
It reminded me that there is light in
even the worst of storms.

I often wonder how Humpty Dumpty
felt when he was broken into
smithereens.
That thought comes to mind when you
tiptoe around eggshells as they glisten
and gleam.
My feelings rapidly change,
A roaring lion, then a nightingale
caught in a golden cage,
You hear of damsels in distress
rescued by knights
But I have it in me to put up my own
fight
If only I could speak the unspoken
word,
Then all this would not sound so
absurd.
Gaslighting has become a norm,
And we all follow it like formless
forms.
If I could change the world one day at
a time,
Aeons from now you and I would
intertwine.

Labels, labels, labels.
They shout as they sit across tables.
"She is an Optimist."
"No a Pessimist."
"No, A Realist."
"No, A Surrealist."
"A Scepticist!" one shouts,
"No a Utopist," the other pouts.
"She has Hysteria" the man frowns,
'We mustn't let her be free in the
town'!
'It's to keep you safe and sound'
They throttle you, so no voice is found
This goes on for a long while;
Then one day fate decides to smile.
The winds begin to change,
Something happened that was so strange.
She rose from the embers,
Like a phoenix from the flames.
The world had now changed,
and she would never be tamed.

The Mother

My home can be a hotel room,
As long as it has the fallen mangoes
from the tree my great great
grandmother planted.
My home can be a hotel room,
As long as the saccharine sweetness
of the Karak tea seduces my nostrils
and taste buds.
My home can be a hotel room.
As long as I have the loving feeling of
almond oil being rubbed on my scalp.
My home can be a hotel room,
As long as it has the ancient purple
stains of Jamun, with its roots holding
me, grounding me, caressing me.
My home can be a hotel room,
As long as my family, and the ones
that hold my heart are there.

Like an old tree that holds the secrets of the past,
Coded in rings and shapes are stories that will last.
Of serpents and dragons slayed by valiant knights,
Droughts, forest fires that stealth in the night.
These images flash before my eyes,
As I touch the parched papers that muffled the cries.
The love letters, the journals, the photos of eras gone by.
They laid the first stone,
I now pave the path.

I feel whole when the muffled sound
of old songs covered by noises of
light conversations and laughter put
me to sleep.
I feel whole when the sound of the
pattering rain hitting my window meets
the noise of the rumbling sky.
I feel whole whilst re-reading a book
that once brought me so much joy.
I feel whole when eating a batch of
cookies my friends and I made
while laughing over the burnt taste.
These moments are my authentic moments
of joy.
These moments are the moments I
look back on: my happy place.

They say smoke is toxic.
They say it's bad for you.
But that smoke is the smoke my dad
and grandfather smoked,
That gave home its scent.
That smoke is the smoke my mother
puts on using the rose incense each
morning,
That she brought with love.
And that smoke is the smoke that
comes from the barbeque my uncle
makes lovingly,
Where memorable moments are
birthed.
So if this is toxicity,
I would have it any day.

I have always wondered about the power
silence held.
Why was it that it was more valued
than communication?
How was it that stillness gave off a
stronger message than anything else?
How was it that it could hold anger,
fear, hatred, grief,
But also joy, gratitude, love and hope?
How does silence stand out?
No, why does silence stand out?
Is it because of the shock that you
can verbalise without talking?
That you can bond without speaking?
Or how different silences could mean
different things, although they sound
the same.
Yes. That is why I marvel at silence.
How it can have a voice without a
mouth.
How it can come in different
languages.

Isn't it ironic?
That the streams of cool water gushing out of the plastic bottle that quenched my thirst,
Is the plastic bottle that suffocated the turtle gasping in bursts?

Isn't it ironic,
That the warm milk in the piping tea that comforts me on cold nights,
Has been savagely and brutally stolen from starving calves who knew it was their right?

Isn't it ironic?
That the one place that is our Mother,
We loot, plunder and destroy with savagery that would make you shudder.

And now dear reader I rest my weary eyes,
My mind gets tired as we hear their screaming cries.
I hope one day we can be part of a fair and just world.
But for now, I trudge daily,
Hoping my efforts will be unfurled.

The Crone

Has an artefact ever told you its
story?
Or was it shunned behind a glass
cage before it could speak its
memory?
Has it ever told you how it got there?
Before it was uprooted from its womb
into this glassware?
Has it ever confessed who was its real
maker?
Who loved it, conceived it and was its
caretaker?
Has it ever shared its tragic
adventures?
Witnessing innocents turn into
avengers?
Or was it silenced?
Just to be unaudienced.
Far away from its home.

It's crazy how a stack of paper can be
a whole universe.
Where the colour blue can taste like
an early morning coffee made by a
loved one,
Or where the sky could smell like wet
paint.
Where happiness can be in the shape
of a peony,
Or where toffee could sound like a
sigh.
And where imagination is a wild
horse,
Finally set free.

They glistened and gleamed like a
polished glass,
Like moonlight reflected on the sea so
vast.
Beyond the horizon the thunder
roared,
Like an army of giant demons
unleashed they poured.
Warm heavy drenching downpour of
monsoon rain,
To take away the heat, to take away
the pain.
I run outside barefoot drowning in
their midst,
Hoping I could evaporate and achieve
the much-needed shift.
But alas I must sit prim and proper
behind the glass doors,
Cuz only savages run barefoot
amongst the shores.
Maybe in another lifetime, I could be
a droplet of rain.
At least that can take away thousands
of years of pain.

I often wonder,
How one doesn't feel small:
In one of the trillions of galaxies,
Where we're a mere piece on a
mosaic wall.
I often wonder,
How something can be so chaotic,
With millions of stars sprawled all
over,
And still, be so perfect.
I often wonder.
How it's possible that my stress
seems to vanish,
Every time I look at the nighttime sky,
Substituting a bandage.
I often wonder,
How each cosmic dust particle fits
together so perfectly;
Like a puzzle fixture,
Making an imperfect yet flawless
picture.
I often wonder.
With microscopic eyes,
The fascinating bursts of colours and
sounds.
Where Galactic babies are birthed and
nucleonic nebula's futures are found.
Space can never stress me out.

Let me tell you a story,
About a creative journey that is both
beautiful and gory.
It was frightening at first,
But there was this inexorable thirst.
I wanted to partake,
In a floodgate of emotions that would
make,
The hardest of hearts melt,
Like steel into soft felt.
But then came the treacherous part,
Where insecurity unleashed like a
bleeding heart.
Did I want everyone to peek in my
past.
Or should I just let this opportunity go
past?
Then one night as I lay pondering
As my mind kept on wandering.
My spirit guide whispered softly,
"Embrace the mess, my love,
That's how your destiny soars above."

If I could be a chameleon,
I would camouflage myself as a tree.
The deepest darkest rainforests would be my canvas,
As I marvel at how peaceful the world around me can be.
If I could be a shooting star,
I would take the journey to the edge of the abyss so so far.
I'd see bursts of colour and creation,
And fireworks that leave me mouth open ajar.
If I could be a Dragon fish,
I would live in the deepest trenches of the ocean.
I'd rule my underwater kingdom with my mighty fin,
Yet tinged with love, benevolence and devotion.
But for now, it seems I am just little old me,
Who reads and marvels at all that could be.
For now, this will have to suffice,
So here I turn back to my imagination to keep me charmed with grains of Paradise.

The torch has been lit,
The flames rise high.
The dye is now cast,
And I sit down with a sigh.

Let me tell you a story,
Of how it all began.
Seemed like an eternity,
Yet in reality only a short time span.

Oh, when it started,
It was just a game.
A road to fortune,
A road to fame.

But I stopped,
Somewhere along the route.
As tenderlings inside of me,
Began to shoot.

I burst out,
As my heart beat fast,
From traversing down valleys,
And mountains, so vast.

Every day was a challenge,
One to reach the next goal,
Yet I stumbled,
As I trudged on my foal.

Then one day,
I stopped to rest.
Took a deep breath,
And I realised that I had given it my best.

And in the journey,
Of high peaks and rivers deep,
I had finally found in my soul,
The rewards I could reap.

It was no longer about winning or losing,
Nor gaining a prize,
I had reached my destination,
And my journey had made me so wise.

www.ingramcontent.com/pod-product-compliance
Lightning Source LLC
LaVergne TN
LVHW020535160826
845677LV00015B/4065